W9-AYI-509

THE GIFT
OF
FORGIVENESS

THE GIFT
OF
FORGIVENESS

OLIVIER CLERC

 FINDHORN PRESS

© Olivier Clerc 2010

The right of Olivier Clerc to be identified as the author
of this work has been asserted by him in accordance
with the Copyright, Designs and Patents Act 1998.

Published in 2010 by Findhorn Press, Scotland

ISBN 978-1-84409-190-4

Edited by Nicky Leach
Cover design by Richard Crookes
Interior design by Damian Keenan
Printed and bound in the USA

Published by
Findhorn Press
117-121 High Street,
Forres IV36 1AB,
Scotland, UK

t +44 (0)1309 690582
f +44 (0)131 777 2711
e info@findhornpress.com

www.findhornpress.com

Contents

Introduction

"You've got a new book to write now!" said Toltec spiritual teacher Don Miguel Ruiz, his steady gaze meeting mine. It was September 1999. We were sitting in the lounge of Villa Teotihuacan, one of five lovely Villas Arqueológicas small hotels adjoining Mayan and Aztec ruins in Mexico. The unique atmosphere of this ancient setting only served to add to the surreal quality of our conversation.

At the time, I didn't quite know what to make of this sweeping, unexpected pronouncement from Don Miguel, a spiritual teacher who interested me greatly but whom I had met for the first time just four days ago at the start of a workshop. It's true that those four days had been filled with life-changing events, and we had shared powerful experiences. Even so, as we met for one last time, the last thing I expected was for Don Miguel to make such a sweeping statement about my future. But, then, I had come to expect the unexpected with Don Miguel.

First, a little background.

I am a longtime Swiss author and translator. At the time of my meeting Don Miguel, I was also the editorial director of a Franco-Swiss publishing house, based in Geneva, Switzerland. It so happened that, while I was in Mexico, the original French version of my latest book—*Modern Medicine: The New World Religion: How Be-*

9

liefs Secretly Influence Medical Dogma and Practices, as it is called in the English-language edition—was just coming off the press in France. Ten years had elapsed since I had last published a book, so I was rather proud and happy to have this new one coming out, and I gladly shared this thrilling news with Don Miguel while we were both enjoying a drink. Needless to say, my next book was about the farthest thing from my mind at that moment.

Picture, then, my reaction when Don Miguel dismissed all of my most recent accomplishments in one swift and enigmatic declaration: "That's already the *past*. You've got a new book to write, now!"

A long, strange route had brought me to Mexico that day, where I was just one of several French-speaking participants at a Toltec workshop led by Don Miguel and his long-term apprentice Maud Séjournant. A French native, Maud was a longtime resident of Santa Fe, New Mexico. It was in Santa Fe that she had met Don Miguel just as he was starting to share his Toltec teachings, and had worked closely with him for a number of years.

At the time of the Mexican trip, I had known Maud for eight years. We initially met in 1991 when I was chief editor for a magazine on spirituality based in Toulouse, France, and hired her to write some articles about Native American wisdom and shamanism. Seven years later, I was working as editorial director for a publishing house in Geneva, Switzerland, when we began discussing a new collaboration. I asked Maud to oversee the publication of a series of English-language books about spirituality, entitled "The Circle of Life," based on the title of her own best-selling French book. My role would be to translate the new series into French and publish the books in Europe.

In the summer of 1998, Maud and I met in the lovely Voirons Mountains near Geneva to discuss which would be the first titles we would publish in the new series. Among the pile of American books she brought with her was a small tome based on Mexican Toltec spiritual teachings that attracted me immediately: *The Four Agreements: A Practical Guide to Personal Freedom*. It was written by an author largely unknown at that time—Don Miguel Ruiz.

The Four Agreements is an extraordinary book. Writing in very simple, modern, and clear language throughout the book, Don Miguel manages to synthesize for Western readers the essence of the Toltec wisdom that has been part of his family's spiritual heritage for generations. The main teaching tool is the use of four simple agreements, which offer a powerful way of working with the thinking patterns and behaviors that keep us unhappy and miserable: "Be impeccable with your word," "Don't take anything personally," "Don't make assumptions," and "Always do your best." These simple yet powerful agreements, if used regularly, are an effective way of creating freedom from fear and access to genuine love—so powerful, in fact, that this small book eventually became a publishing phenomenon and a worldwide bestseller.

I spent the whole night reading the book and became full of enthusiasm for its clear and true message. I was particularly drawn to its practical approach to daily life. Moreover, even though the book's sales were still modest in the United States, its sales potential in Europe was immediately obvious to me. The very next day, I contacted the American agent of the publisher, Amber-Allen Publishing, and requested the French rights. I didn't waste a moment getting started on the translation on my return to Geneva. The book had been published just a couple of months before my trip to Mexico.

I often say I don't publish books; I publish *authors*. I like to meet the people behind the printed page. That's especially true in the fields of self-help, spirituality, New Age, and shamanism. These are areas that interest me greatly. For me, it is of the utmost importance that authors I publish "walk their talk," as Native Americans say, and I often make a point of checking out an author's work by attending their workshops. Shortly before meeting Don Miguel Ruiz, I trained with Marshall Rosenberg, founder of Nonviolent Communication (NVC). Likewise back in 1983, I trained in North Carolina with Robert Monroe, author of *Out of Body Experiences*. I did the same with various well-known European authors.

After reading *The Four Agreements*, it wasn't out of character for me at all to feel a strong desire to meet the man behind these fascinating teachings. I wanted to experience for myself the truth of his message and the energy of love that permeates his writing. When Maud called to tell me she was organizing a special two-week French-speaking Toltec workshop with Don Miguel in Mexico and New Mexico, I immediately signed up. The plan was that we would train with Don Miguel at Teotihuacan the first week, then decamp to New Mexico for additional training with Maud and another longtime Toltec apprentice of Don Miguel, Brandt Morgan. When I found out that the first day of the workshop coincided with my 38th birthday, I took it as a sign that I should make this journey both to Mexico and within myself. It's funny, isn't it, how we often find "signs" that confirm the very choices we are already set on making?

So it was that I found myself in Mexico in 1999, for a two-week trip that would have a far-reaching impact on my whole life—an impact I couldn't possibly have foreseen.

During the five days I spent with Don Miguel in Mexico, I went through one of the most extraordinary experiences of my whole life. Since then, I have used the unique teaching I received from him again and again. The seed for the book you hold in your hands was sown then and there and has quietly taken root over the years. Now, a decade later, after the American publication of two of my other books, it feels finally as though the time is ripe for this book.

The teaching on the Gift of Forgiveness that Don Miguel gave me and other workshop participants in Mexico and encouraged me to share with others has not been included in any of his other books. But it has had such a major impact on my life that I believe it would be a shame if it were known only to those of us who were there that week. Teachings such as this are meant to be passed on. I have often informally shared with others the principles of what I learned that week. By writing this book, I hope to offer the world what Don Miguel so generously offered me, and also to thank him from the bottom of my heart for this invaluable gift.

May you find the inner peace and love that this Gift of Forgiveness brings forth.

Olivier Clerc, September 2009

CHAPTER 1

An Unforgettable Encounter

We were a group of approximately 20 people from France and Switzerland, gathered by Maud Séjournant to participate in a unique workshop with Don Miguel Ruiz in Teotihuacan, Mexico. The workshop was to be simultaneously translated into French, for those of us who spoke neither English nor Spanish, the two languages Don Miguel uses when teaching.

We all took the same flight to Mexico City, enjoyed two free days in that huge city, then took a bus to our small hotel near the ancient site of Teotihuacan, where Don Miguel was to join us. In addition to me, there were the chief staff workshop leader for the famous Intercontinental hotel chain in Paris, the human resources manager of the French computer company Bull, and the most reputable psychotherapist in Grenoble. We were a high-powered group. During those first two days, it was natural that would all interact with each other wearing our "social masks."

On our first evening at Villa Teotihuacan, we were told to gather in the hotel meeting room to meet Don Miguel. From across the room, I saw him arrive, greet Maud, and start talking with her. His physical appearance was quite ordinary—jeans, an old colored shirt over a T-shirt—but I immediately *felt* his presence in the room, like if something was radiating silently from him, from a distance. At some point, they both looked in my direction. I gathered Maud was telling Don Miguel that I was the French translator of his books *The Four Agreements* and *Mastery of Love*, part of her own series of books that I was publishing in France. After she had finished telling him about me, Don Miguel beckoned me over.

What happened next was my first tantalizing taste of what was to come over the next five days.

My eagerness probably showed all over my face as I hastened across the room to be introduced to Don Miguel in the flesh. He looked at me, with a smile on his face, and wrapped me in a big warm embrace. To onlookers, the meeting would have appeared commonplace. A simple everyday greeting. Nothing unique or special. No loud drum roll to capture everyone's attention. Nothing. *Nada.* But I can tell you this: When Don Miguel looked at me, when he took me in his arms—no matter how ordinary it may have seemed on the outside—I experienced a powerful shift in my whole being. The communication between us was powerful. I felt seen. I felt acknowledged. I felt unconditionally loved.

I was stunned. It felt as if the burden of a lifetime had been lifted from my shoulders. I felt recognized for who I really was, deep inside, in a way I'd never known. Suddenly, all the projections and judgments from others I had carried simply dropped away.

Many people talk or write about "unconditional love"; many try to practice it. In my experience, though, it is often the very teachers and trainers who believe themselves to be living springs of unconditional love who confuse the feeling of deep contentment and self-satisfaction they derive from their personal success and power over others for "unconditional love." Before my encounter with Don Miguel, I had witnessed more "love of power" than "power of love."

During the brief exchange between Don Miguel and me, no words were uttered. Yet his whole attitude, his whole being, "spoke" to me more powerfully than any words ever could. And I heard his message—not with my ears and brain but with my heart and every single cell of my body. Actually, I'm not even sure Miguel gave me a message at all. It would probably be more accurate to say that he embodied the message. It was as if he were a piece of beautiful music—his way of living expresses such a different tone, such a different melody than what we are accustomed to experiencing in someone. Intentional or not, Don Miguel's very vibration can't help but draw others into a lasting resonance with his.

Please understand: In writing this, I do not mean to idealize Don Miguel, to turn him into some kind of demi-god. In my life, I have been lucky enough to meet many remarkable people, each possessing unique knowledge, capacities, and gifts. All were human, no doubt about that. All had their limits, their blind spots, and their shortcomings. But Don Miguel embodied a unique quality of love. I felt it not only during our first meeting but throughout the whole workshop. All of us did. It was an experience of love that lingered in our hearts for many months afterwards.

Don Miguel's loving energy had an immediate impact on everyone. Within a couple of hours, we had dropped our "social masks" and had returned to our fundamental humanity, to something beneath the personas we humans adopt to hide our true nature from view.

By the time we turned in for the night, we were no longer a collection of separate individuals, caught up in our egos; we were a real group, with intimate connections and interactions, sharing a deeper level of communication than many of us had experienced with people we had known for years.

My own experience of the way Don Miguel caused a shift in relationships is very telling. In Mexico City, on our first two days of sightseeing, I had been assigned to share a double room with another workshop participant, Gérard, with whom I felt little affinity. Gérard, a tall handsome guy in his early fifties, worked in the computer business. He looked like a very rational man, more interested in hard facts and sciences than in anything emotional or spiritual. Actually, I even wondered what this guy was doing on the trip, he seemed so at odds with the purpose of this workshop. Yes, I know—judgments. I was already breaking the first of Don Miguel's Four Agreements: "Be impeccable with your word." Now, at Villa Teotihuacan, I found myself again sharing a room with Gérard. But after that first memorable evening in Don Miguel's company, something had changed between Gérard and me. A friendship was born that has only grown stronger over the past 10 years, for which I remain very thankful. I never thought that two people from such different worlds could ever have anything more than a nice, social, and polite relationship. I was wrong.

I had come to the Land of the Toltecs to verify what kind of man was behind the beautiful message in Don Miguel's books. The answer came that very first evening in Teotihuacan. But there was plenty more to come…

CHAPTER 2

The Crystal Jaguar

The next morning, Don Miguel started leading us on a five-day "spiritual pilgrimage" through the various Toltec monuments of Teotihuacan. It is a sacred Toltec ritual that Don Miguel has offered numerous groups over the years, carried out in successive daily stages, leading finally to the top of the Pyramid of the Sun. I will not recount that journey here. Others have already done an excellent job of describing it in earlier books. I strongly recommend *Beyond Fear: A Toltec Guide to Freedom and Joy* by Mary Carroll Nelson, written with Don Miguel Ruiz.

In the evening, after a delicious Mexican dinner, we reassembled in the meeting room at Villa Teotihuacan. This evening, no sooner were we seated than Don Miguel asked me to stand and walk to the front of the group. I was surprised and had no idea what to expect. Then, he offered me a beautiful little crystal jaguar similar to those on sale in shops around Teotihuacan.

"Do you know why I'm making this present to you?" Don Miguel asked.

"Because I had my birthday upon arriving in Mexico?" I answered, the only reason I could imagine for the gift.

Now, wasn't that a clever guess ? Don Miguel is such a fine man he makes gifts to workshop participants whose birthday happens to fall on the dates of any given workshop! Isn't that nice?

Wrong. That wasn't it at all.

"No," replied Don Miguel. "I'm offering you this crystal jaguar because I'm taking you as my apprentice. You are now a Jaguar Knight."

Well, I certainly didn't expect that. It didn't figure in my plans at all.

As opposed to the other participants, I wasn't here to become a "Jaguar," as apprentices are called in the Toltec tradition Don Miguel observes. Indeed, I was the only participant *not* to have brought a wooden stick, a red cloth, two feathers, and two small crystals to be made into a power stick by Toltec mentor Brandt Morgan in New Mexico. No, I had come to Mexico to meet Don Miguel, hoping to receive some valuable teachings and to have a powerful experience with him; I had no intention of dedicating myself to that particular spiritual path, however wonderful and valuable I found it to be. I already have my own spiritual path. Sure, I remain open to other ideas—I'm incurably eclectic—but I had no interest in adopting another belief system.

More to the point: As we started our editorial work together, Maud had told me quite clearly that Don Miguel had stopped taking new apprentices. From then on, only fully certified Toltec mentors—people such as Maud Séjournant, Brandt Morgan, and others—would train apprentices. So, it had never even crossed my mind that I might become Miguel's apprentice, nor was it even my wish to do so.

I was taken aback by Don Miguel's invitation and over-whelmed by mixed emotions. On the one hand, I was undeniably moved by Miguel's gift and his invitation to apprentice with him. Like our first encounter, I took it as a sign of recognition, all the more precious since it came from someone for whom I felt deep appreciation and admiration.

On the other hand—for lack of sufficient spiritual maturity, perhaps—I was afraid that if I accepted his offer it might represent some sort of "betrayal" of my own spiritual lineage. Only now do I realize that these two spiritual paths, albeit in different cultural forms, are actually very similar. If I had decided to devote part of my energy and time to this Toltec apprenticeship, it would certainly not have conflicted at all with my other spiritual beliefs.

Finally, my ego was torn between feelings of pride for being suddenly the "chosen one" in this group and, I must confess, a certain annoyance at Don Miguel for announcing his decision to take me as his apprentice in front of the whole group. I thought he should at least have asked me ahead of time whether I wanted to do this. ("Who does he think he is, anyway?") My ego had not been consulted, you see!

At the time, I was too uptight or timid to share these feelings with Don Miguel. Perhaps I was afraid he might judge me conceited for not realizing what an invaluable gift he was bestowing on me. (Miguel judging me? Now, there's a projection!) So, I didn't say anything that night, nor later on during the workshop. Soon, wrapped in Don Miguel's simple love and appreciation, and the warmth and security of the group, I let my negative feelings go and just enjoyed the positive aspects of this powerful moment.

But these not-so-shiny emotions did not vanish. There were to be consequences in my life, both during this trip and shortly afterwards, when I got back to France. Indeed, a week later, in

New Mexico, when Toltec mentor Brandt Morgan performed the power-stick ceremony for the participants who wished to become "Jaguars," I was asked to lend my crystal jaguar to be used in the ceremony. I gladly complied. But when the jaguar was returned to me, at the end of the ritual, one of its legs was broken. I couldn't help but see this as a sign of my ambiguous feelings towards Don Miguel's offer and his gift to me.

Back home in France, I managed to glue together the jaguar's broken leg. I placed it with various spiritual objects in a little altar on top of my piano. Among the objects there was a beautiful and precious ancient Tibetan statue that had been with me for more than 20 years. It was one of the only objects to which I was attached—not because of its financial value but because of the astonishingly graceful posture of the deity it represents.

A couple of weeks later, while I was at work, my house was burglarized. When I came home, I was surprised to find I could not open the front door. I soon discovered marks in the wooden door jamb suggesting somebody had forced their way inside the house. I went out to the garden, found an open window—the same one the burglar had used to leave the house—and climbed inside.

Very few things had actually been stolen. The burglar had taken the keys of my motor scooter and driven it away. As it turned out, this was good news. I had just been told by my mechanic that this motor scooter had a lot more mileage than the odometer showed and that I had obviously been cheated by the guy who'd sold it to me. The insurance allowed me to have a much better one afterwards. My old laptop had also been stolen. There again, this was good news. I had been thinking of buying a new one and I had backed up all my important files. The only other thing taken, strangely enough, was my little crystal jaguar. It had almost no monetary value: its main significance was that it was the repository of my mixed feelings about becoming Don Miguel's apprentice. Meanwhile, my beloved Tibetan statue was still there. It still stands on my desk as I write these lines.

I decided to take this theft as final proof that my inner link with Don Miguel would remain subtle and spiritual. A powerful connection of love. It did not need to take material form—be it a crystal jaguar or written documents, such as those that were supposed to be sent to me as his apprentice but which I never actually received.

And, as it turned out, it was not the moment that Don Miguel invited me to be his apprentice that would be his greatest teaching and gift to me. It was the moment right afterwards.

CHAPTER 3

The Gift of Forgiveness

I was still feeling confused by Don Miguel's invitation to apprentice with him, when he asked me to kneel in front of Véronique, one of the other participants. She was seated just a couple of feet away from me, at one end of the long benches on either side of our large meeting room.

"Ask her to forgive you," Don Miguel instructed.

I was extremely puzzled by this. Had I wronged this woman in some way that Don Miguel had perceived and I hadn't? My mind went into overdrive. I did a mental run-through of all that had happened over the past three days. As I did so, I realized that I had not yet established a warm, friendly bond with this woman. We hadn't yet made a real connection. Something in her was probably pushing some of my inner buttons. This was the only reason I could bring to mind to explain Don Miguel's unusual request. So, I just swallowed my pride and did as I was told. I knelt in front of Véronique.

"Please forgive me, " I started saying, "for not having … "

Before I could finish my sentence, Don Miguel interrupted me.

"Just ask for forgiveness," he instructed. "Don't add anything."

I stopped in mid-sentence, somewhat disconcerted.

"And then," Miguel added, "do the same thing with the next person, and the next, until you've come full circle with all the people present in the room."

Wow. What a request! I was going to have to ask for forgiveness on my knees from more than 20 people, including Maud and her assistant. Having to do that with just one person was already difficult—but a whole group?

Confronted with this unexpected situation, which stirred powerful feelings and emotions in me, my mind went blank. I stopped thinking altogether. It was only much later, when I had finished, that I realized that Miguel had told me to ask for forgiveness from Véronique only because she was the first one seated on that end of the bench, thus being closest to me. It wasn't because anything particular had happened between her and me.

Here, then, was the third of the Four Agreements: "Don't make assumptions."

And so, still kneeling, I shuffled sideways to the person next to Véronique. Again—but this time without trying to find a particular reason—I said, "Please forgive me," while looking straight into the eyes of that participant. Then I moved to the next person. "Please forgive me." And the next. "Please forgive me."

The more times I did this, the more I found myself slowly moving into a different state of consciousness. As I knelt in front of each of them, my fellow participants looked at me with love, understanding, and compassion in their eyes.

They were all very different people, from all walks of life, with an age range of more than 30 years separating the youngest and oldest. Suddenly, I felt and understood—not only with my heart and brain but at a gut level—that by asking for forgiveness from all of these different strangers, I was actually asking for forgiveness from all the people I had known in my life, and even beyond.

I was not merely asking to be forgiven by one person in particular, but to be forgiven by everyone I might have hurt in my lifetime, with the group representing a kind of global healing community. Each participant was like a window, a symbol, or a hub, through which my request was being transmitted to hundreds or thousands of others, worldwide, while I, in return, received the forgiving look and smile of all these people. It was almost like asking for forgiveness from all mankind.

My defenses were falling one after the other. The judgments I had made about anyone, anywhere, were disintegrating, becoming meaningless. I was feeling waves of love surge through my whole being. By the time I reached the end of the circle, I was having a peak experience, feeling completely high, without having consumed anything but this elixir of forgiveness.

But it wasn't finished yet.

Don Miguel asked me to stand up and come to him.

"Now," he said, "ask for forgiveness from the Devil."

My mind was no longer in charge. Without a thought, I just did what I was asked to do, silently, within myself.

"Then, ask for forgiveness from God," Don Miguel went on.

Again, I went deep within myself. By this time, it had become quite easy. I asked God to forgive me.

"Last, and most difficult, too," said Miguel. "Ask for forgiveness from yourself."

By now I could feel the truth of his words fully. Our greatest judge is not God—or rather the image of God each one of us creates in our own mind—but ourselves. If all my defenses, all my judgments, had not already been greatly diminished by the steps leading up to this one, I don't think self-forgiveness, the true heart of forgiveness, would have been possible. So, in my mind, I said to myself "Please, forgive me!" one last time. I immediately felt a huge sensation of inner relief, a feeling of total surrender and let go. It was as if the last knot that kept me bound to my judgments, grudges, and grievances was finally cut. The cage of my heart at last broke open, and I felt free to love and be loved. It was like being reborn.

"We use others," Don Miguel explained, "we use the Devil, God, and most of all ourselves, to hurt ourselves, to stop ourselves from loving, and to let ourselves be trapped in fear and judgments. We refuse to forgive *them* for what we think *they* have done to *us*, when actually it is we who have judged them. Because of our judgments, we have stopped loving them. And when we stop loving one person, we reduce the flow of love pouring out of our heart. So, it is *we* who need to ask for forgiveness from *them,* and not the other way around. We ask others to forgive us for having used them to shut ourselves off from love, while blaming them for our own choice."

Then, Don Miguel had everyone in the group form a circle around the two of us, to create a tight human pack filled with love and compassion. I felt as naked as a newborn baby, stripped of the layer upon layer of fear that had armored my heart over the years. I truly felt able to love and be loved, maybe for the first time in my life. I felt extremely vulnerable without these long-held defenses, yet very strong and alive—my energy being no longer consumed by an overprotecting ego. I felt both exhausted and relieved. Mostly, I felt deeply grateful to Don Miguel for having given me, and the whole group, this wonderful and powerful Gift of Forgiveness.

"You can use this method again, by yourself, whenever you need it," Don Miguel later told us. "You don't have to have anyone present by your side. During your meditation—eyes closed, deep within yourself—just visualize the people from whom you need to ask for forgiveness, and do exactly as you've done tonight, always ending by asking for forgiveness from the Devil, from God, and from yourself. And it will work. You will free yourself of all judgments, you will be cleansed, and your heart will love again without restriction."

The Gift of Forgiveness *is* powerful, just as our introduction to it was that night in Mexico. Three other participants in our group share their reactions to the experience here:

٭

For the past ten years, this moment has remained intact in my memory, as if engraved by the powerfully associated emotions.

We barely knew each other, and suddenly Olivier knelt down and pronounced this strange and marvelous sentence, "Please, forgive me!"

Time stopped.

I was both surprised and deeply moved by the beauty and purity of this timeless moment, which was to be repeated in front of each one of us. I was crying, like many others, without knowing why.

It is only later on, once the emotion wore off, that I understood why: it was so beautiful and so powerful! What a reversal! An exit from the state of victim. And back to our full responsibility, restoring our true divine filiation. I AM RESPONSIBLE FOR WHAT I HAVE CREATED.

How could I ever forget such a powerful realization?

It changed my perception of the events of my life and it helped me a great deal in all my relationships with others.

Forgiveness has become a key, and no longer an act of contrition.

Sylvie Tarlet

✺

This particular moment in our experience with Don Miguel Ruiz left a powerful impression on me. At the beginning of the session, I felt awkward. My mind rebelled that Olivier should have to ask forgiveness like this, on his knees, in what looked almost like a humiliating posture. I reflected about how much guilt religion usually conveys, in relation to forgiving.

Then, the further he went through the process, kneeling down in front of each person and asking forgiveness, the more I had the feeling that the connection between us all was becoming palpable, almost material. The only present thing that mattered became this dimension of universal love, far beyond anything mental, which every single part of my being could feel. The other aspects—all the participants' characters and differences—became of secondary importance.

Time had stopped and I was aware of going through a major experience, even though I couldn't understand it, intellectually speaking, at the time.

What has remained with me, of this particular moment and of these days spent with Don Miguel Ruiz?

I think it was my first encounter—ever—with Love. I was opening myself to this dimension in a real-life context. I was discovering this Love that underlies all the forms that love can take afterwards. The source of love. After this workshop, I have always described Don Miguel as just a big "ball of love." That's exactly what he radiates through his simple presence.

Later on, through my various searches and discoveries, I ended up understanding intellectually what happened on this famous day. Today, I see a close link between the Gift of Forgiveness and the Hawaiian practice of Ho'oponopono which "simply" suggests to ask forgiveness and love all of our sick aspects, often mirrored by the people we meet. Forgiveness opens the door to inclusion and non-rejection. Thus, practicing forgiveness makes us free and provides us with a healing.

I now practice this on a daily basis, and it keeps illuminating my life.

Virginie Pré

❖

Olivier was right in wondering what a guy like me was doing in this workshop! I often wondered myself, at least during the first week. I was a Martian landing on another planet, or like a guy from the countryside arriving in Paris, …or rather the other way 'round!

Many messages from Don Miguel went literally over my head, in particular the ritual marvelously described by Olivier in these pages. "What is this thing where we have to kneel down to ask forgiveness from everybody? Will I have to go through this myself ???" I wondered.

This book illuminates this ritual and gives it back its full meaning, along with its associated process of forgiveness. It has helped me better understand this fantastic tool, to the point where I tried this ritual the very evening I read the book. Even though I did get a little bit mixed up in the process, the result is clearly there and I will do it again in the days to come.

The names of people that came to me were mostly those I felt I had done harm to, not those who might have done wrong to me! Strangely enough, I couldn't find anyone I felt had done harm to me!

Sometimes, I feel I didn't even take 10% of what Don Miguel gave us during those days in Mexico. And even 10%, I'm not sure… but it has been a one way trip for me. Upon returning, I wasn't the same person. An impulse had made me totally change direction! It was the second major 'inflexion' in my life, since I was born, and—just as the first one—at the time I was totally unaware of it.

Now, with a 10-year perspective, I can really assess what a major change it has brought in my life!

Gérard Meyer

CHAPTER 4

Afterthoughts on the Gift of Forgiveness

The process Don Miguel had me go through was so intense, especially in a group context, that it was only later that I had a chance to reflect on what it meant. I lived this experience fully, with my whole being, carried away by powerful feelings and emotions that left little room for my mind's otherwise restless activity.

The next morning, I awoke with a definite sensation of having changed my center of gravity. I felt more grounded, less in my head, and a lot calmer. I used to have a tendency to swallow my meals very rapidly. Now I found myself suddenly eating slowly, without effort, enjoying every bite of food much more than before. I felt myself more alive, more in touch with others, my mind less likely to carry me away to other places, to other times, past and future. I felt more present.

Once I was back home and had chance to reflect on the experience at Teotihuacan, I realized that one of the keys to this Toltec Gift of Forgiveness is a complete reversal of our usual understanding of how things work, and, hence, of our actions, with regard to forgiveness.

Let me try to explain.

All of us have been hurt and wounded at some point in our

lives—some of us, many times—and we may feel a lot of resentment, anger, even hatred towards the people who were responsible. Our religious education may have taught us "to forgive our enemies" or "to turn the other cheek," but we may find it very difficult to do so, even if we're willing. Merely thinking about forgiving someone rarely works. Forgiveness comes from the heart and, as French philosopher Blaise Pascal wrote in the 17th century, "The heart has reasons that reason cannot know."

Feelings do not yield to our will; they have a life and a flow of their own. So, try as we might, we may find ourselves unable to muster a genuine feeling of forgiveness for someone "who's done us wrong." Consequently, we may feel torn between our willingness to forgive and our inability to do so, and we may feel guilty for having feelings of resentment and rage. It becomes a vicious cycle. The more we try to push ourselves in the direction of forgiveness ("I *must* forgive them"), the more we trigger resistance in our heart, and the more we blame ourselves for it.

We may feel we are morally in the right, that the other person just doesn't deserve our forgiveness, that we cannot forgive them for what they have done. In effect, we feel superior to them. We are good; they are bad. We become like a king, a governor, a president, a judge, someone who has the right to grant a pardon to a condemned person. We revel in the power we believe we have over others.

The practice of the Gift of Forgiveness changes our mental script. We are no longer seated on the throne of our ego. We no longer weigh whether to show largesse and forgive those who have maliciously hurt us, judging whether these people deserve to be forgiven. Instead, we become aware of our own judgments. We realize how these judgments have led us to close off our heart and to hurt ourselves even more, using whatever other people may have done to us as justification. Using the practice of the Gift of Forgiveness, *we* ask forgiveness from *them.*

What's happening here? Why does this work?

In choosing to ask for forgiveness, we move from a place of self-importance and pride to a place of humility. We drop our pretense, climb down from our ivory tower, and something opens up inside us. By shedding our armor and our grievances, we are free again. Remember Don Miguel's words: The most important part of asking for forgiveness isn't related to others; it's related to ourselves and to the merciless judgments we so promptly pass on ourselves. ("I shall never forgive myself for having done ... been ... said ... that.") Since learning this practice, I no longer try to forgive myself for whatever I've done—the things that my inner judge has condemned; instead, I humbly ask for forgiveness from myself. When I do this, the bill of indictment and all the charges I had made against myself just melt away.

The main purpose of the Gift of Forgiveness is to restore the flow of love in our heart, which has been reduced—or frozen altogether—after the various hurts we've experienced. When we stop loving, we are the first to suffer. We become cold, dry, and defensive. We lose part of our natural joy.

In asking for forgiveness from others, the purpose is *not* to become great friends with people who've done bad things to us, but to stop shutting down our hearts and imprisoning ourselves in resentment, anger, and other isolating feelings. We don't have to actively love our enemies, or even like them; we just need to stop shutting down our capacity to love them, to stop using them as a reason for shrinking our hearts and progressively drying up our love. That's a major difference.

When we work to open our hearts, be able to love, be humble, and ask for forgiveness, it doesn't mean that we stop being discerning, as some people seem to believe. Indeed, in the name of "nonjudgment"—a very fashionable value, these days—too many people mistakenly also set aside their discriminating mind. In reclaiming their hearts, their feelings, their emotions, their compassion, some people tend to reject their analytical mind and intellectual faculties.

This is not what is being asked of us when we practice nonjudgment. Since we have both a heart and an intellect, it is obvious that we need both in order to function effectively. The world today reflects many of the negative consequences of an intellect not tempered by the heart: cynicism, coldness, incivility, ruthless exploitation of others and nature, and other sadly familiar behaviors. But a heart not counterbalanced by the analytical mind is little better. It opens the door to illusions, poorly informed choices, the risk of being manipulated for gain, and other problems.

The Gift of Forgiveness is intended to help us free ourselves of our judging mind, not of our discernment. The Gift of Forgiveness can free our heart from the prison of our fears, anger, and resentment. But it doesn't mean, once the door is open, that we have to let everyone in, indiscriminately. That's where discernment comes in.

The Gift of Forgiveness, in short, is an exceptional tool, but it is neither an all-in-one Swiss Army knife that will help you solve *all* your problems nor a quick-fix solution that you can use anytime, anywhere. There are no such solutions, despite what many self-help books and workshops try to make us believe. Remember American psychologist Abraham Maslow's beautiful piece of advice: "To those who only have a hammer, all problems look like nails." A hammer is a wonderful tool, but we also need a screwdriver, a pair of pliers, a saw, and so on. Think of the Gift of Forgiveness, then, as a well-designed tool. It will occupy a place in your personal toolbox for inner work; but keep adding other tools to the toolbox, to help you handle all kinds of situations and problems.

CHAPTER 5

How to Use the
Gift of Forgiveness

The Gift of Forgiveness practice I learned from Don Miguel Ruiz in Mexico continued to bring lasting benefit to me for nearly three months after my trip. Slowly, though, I realized some old behavior patterns were returning: judgments were beginning to creep in, and my heart was no longer as open as it was during my trip to Teotihuacan. It was time for me to do some inner cleansing, to take down the walls that my intellect was surreptitiously rebuilding, negative thought by negative thought, around the loving spring of my heart.

Don Miguel had told us we could use the Gift of Forgiveness any time we needed it, once we returned home. So, one night, before going to sleep, I decided to practice it on my own, comfortably sitting in a lotus position on my bed.

First, I took some time to meditate, to free myself from the thoughts and worries of the day, and to reach a state of inner calm. Then, I visualized the first person from whom I wanted to ask for forgiveness. I allowed myself to reexperience the tensions that existed between us: the judgments I held against her, the feelings that tended to come up for me as soon as I thought about her, my self-righteousness about the problems that existed between us. I could feel both in my heart and in my body all the stressful sensations and emotions that were overwhelming me all over again. I could see how this tension between us was impairing me, diminishing my capacity to love and feel good.

Then, when I felt ready, I asked of this person in my mind, from the bottom of my heart, "Please, forgive me."

As I did this, I took the time to notice how it really felt in my body to ask for forgiveness: I could feel my muscles suddenly relaxing (particularly my jaw, neck, and shoulders), my solar plexus opening up, the softening sensation of letting go of my grievances, the humbling yet expansive feeling of no longer considering myself superior nor in a position to bestow my own forgiveness on that person. I felt the profound relief that comes from no longer judging, from opening the doors to that part of my heart that I had closed, feeling once more the natural pulse and flow of love within it, free from the prison bars that kept me captive.

Since I was alone and visualizing real people about whom I had negative feelings—not people who acted as substitutes, as was the case at Teotihuacan—I was able to take my time asking for forgiveness from each person. I would continue until I felt a sense of completion with one person. Then, I would go on to the next person and do the same thing all over again, until I felt complete with everyone on my list. With each person, I started with big issues, major conflicts, then moved on to minor ones and seemingly unimportant situations. Now that the process had started I felt the need to complete it, until every negative emotion had been addressed.

When I was done with all the people I could think of, I went on to ask for forgiveness from the Devil. I realized how easy it is to use "dark forces" or "negative energies" as a pretext for sticking to a position of superiority and holding back my love. It is a common trap when navigating the field of self-help, New Age, and spirituality, where we may be tempted to view ourselves as "warriors of light," aligned with the "forces of good." Such self-identifications can be used to justify a personal battle against the "dark side of the force"—perhaps in the form of a partner or a boss—and our hearts can turn cold as we fight our own personal holy war. At such times, I find it useful to keep in mind the Chinese saying: "Don't fight darkness; just bring in light." In the face of evil and hatred, it is more important to keep our hearts alive and loving than to do battle with dark forces.

Next, I asked for forgiveness from God. Here, too, it is tempting to hold negative feelings towards whatever our representation may be of that which is beyond us, no matter what we call it: the Source, the Energy, the Cosmic Intelligence at work in the Universe and in our own lives. When things don't turn out the way we wish, when trials and ordeals come our way, when sorrow and grief show up in our existence, we may blame it on God, on the Great Order of things, and let ourselves feel victimized and resentful of divine influence. By doing this, though, we effectively shut ourselves off from divine love, sever our connection with higher energies, and are the first to suffer because of our alienation from the divine source. But in asking for forgiveness from God, we restore that connection, that living and loving link. We once again feel part of the Universe, interconnected with the great web of life.

The most important stage in the Gift of Forgiveness came last, as I asked for forgiveness from myself. When I first started working with the Gift or Forgiveness, I found this quite difficult. My inner judge was harsh, demanding, uncompromising. I sometimes felt totally unworthy of ever being forgiven.

Perhaps I felt afraid that if I stopped putting all this pressure on myself, and freed myself from the merciless inner tyrant inside me, his constant threats might come true: "You'll never amount to anything ," "You're no good," "You're just a drifter," and other criticisms.

In my experience, just the opposite happens. When I manage to forgive myself, to let go of my self-judgments, to take the pressure off myself, I am much more able to open up, to thrive, to give and receive love in a way that promotes new possibilities and enhances all my relationships. I actually find that when I reach that final stage of self-forgiveness, I can breathe a big inner sigh of relief. It's as if a surgical clamp has at last been removed from the valves of my heart, so that love can now flow freely, at full speed and volume.

When the whole process of the Gift of Forgiveness was finished that night, most of my muscular tensions—both in my body and my face—had disappeared, proof that my inner stress and judgments were all gone. The next morning, I woke up rejuvenated, light, and fresh. For me, doing this practice just before going to bed ensures that the process will deepen during sleep and that my subconscious will integrate this new mind-set (and "heart-set," as well). I find this to be the case each time. I feel open. I feel younger. I feel a great sense of wellbeing.

If you wish to start practicing the Gift of Forgiveness yourself, here are the steps I suggest, based on the practice I learned from Don Miguel and my own experience:

STEP 1:
Creating a Space for Yourself

If you do this during the day, find a quiet place where you are sure to be undisturbed for anything from a half-hour to a full hour. Unplug or turn off your phone(s). Find a comfortable position. You may sit on a chair, move into a meditation posture, or even prostrate yourself or kneel on the floor, as Don Miguel had me do in Teotihuacan. Never underestimate the power of body postures: they are a language of their own and carry a strong meaning. If you kneel down, or if you fully prostrate yourself, you will move even more rapidly into a feeling of humility, you will physically feel a readiness and willingness to ask for forgiveness.

STEP 2:
Reaching Inner Stillness

If you are familiar with a relaxation or meditation technique, whatever it is, use it to reach inner stillness. If you don't know any techniques, just close your eyes and, for a couple of minutes, slowly focus on your inhale and exhale breaths as they enter and leave your body. The object is to create space inside you, so that you can transition between the thoughts and worries of the day and the inner process you are about to start. Within a few minutes, your breath will slow down and your mental chatter will diminish. Thoughts will still inevitably flow through.

That's natural. Don't try to stop them, just notice them and let them go, and gently come back to focusing on your breath. Now, you are ready to practice the Gift of Forgiveness.

STEP 3:
Ask for Forgiveness from Others

Once you are fully relaxed and quiet inside, visualize the first person from whom you want to ask for forgiveness. There is no special order to follow. Just choose the first person who comes to mind. Let yourself become aware of the tensions, conflicts, and/or negative feelings that have caused you to shut off your heart from that person. Don't dwell on this, though. Immediately afterwards, in your mind's eye, look that person in the eyes and sincerely ask for their forgiveness by silently saying: "Please, forgive me." Let go of your grievances, let go of the tensions that block the flow of your heart, as soon as you see that person or think of them. Let go of your position of superiority, of your self-righteousness, and become aware of what you lose by closing off your heart. Then, feel in your whole body what you now gain by reopening it and freeing the natural flow of your love.

Once you feel the process is finished with that person, once you sense something has unlocked and changed within you, move on to the next person who comes to mind, and repeat this step. Sometimes it will only take a minute, sometimes it will take longer, depending on what relationship you have with that particular individual. Feel free to take as much or as little time as you feel is necessary. You don't need to do this process with all the people with whom you have issues in the space of one session; repeat the process another time, and work through as many of your personal relationships as you like in each session.

The first time, or the first few times, you practice the Gift of Forgiveness, you may find you have a long list of people to check off, some of whom may have been absent from your present life a while, or may even be deceased. Eventually, there will come a point when you only have to work with present and relatively recent conflicts and tensions, so that the whole process will take much less time to complete.

When you feel you are finished with asking for forgiveness from others, at least for today, move on to the next step.

STEP 4:
Asking for Forgiveness from
the Devil and from God

We not only blame others for having closed off our own hearts, we also blame it on the Devil and on God.

By asking for forgiveness from the Devil—however strange that may seem to you, at first—you are actually reclaiming the power you gave over to "dark forces" or other "negative energies." Only you can stop the flow of love in your heart. When you say "Please, forgive me" to the Devil—or to whatever form the counter or negative forces may take for you—you release yourself from the grip you've allowed them to have on your heart. You recover your full capacity to love, in spite of the negativity you may find in the world and around you. Yes, evil things do happen in this world; that is a reality. And evil things may even have happened to you, personally. But that doesn't automatically turn you into a victim *forced* to shut your heart.

Practicing the Gift of Forgiveness isn't meant to have a direct impact on others, although indirectly it will; it is designed to work first and foremost on you, on your openness, on what makes you—unconsciously, most of the time—decide where, when, and towards whom or what you will be loving. It helps us reframe our reasons for suddenly turning off the faucet of our loving energy. If you stay open and capable of love, you will influence others and, in this way, the Gift of Forgiveness does have an indirect impact on the people around you.

Now, ask for forgiveness from God, or from whatever form you give to that Higher Intelligence, Source, Destiny, or Cosmic Energy, no matter your beliefs, which guides and rules your life. Because yes, indeed, we also use God as an excuse to close ourselves down in times of difficulty, trials, and ordeals. We resign ourselves to our fate. We arch our back against destiny. We see life as unfair. We feel resentment and frustration.

Certainly, we may not dare to express these feelings openly, for fear of divine consequences. After all, even after 2,000 years of Christianity, the idea of God as a universal loving father figure hasn't yet trumped that older, wrathful, and vengeful God portrayed in the Old Testament. But when we say to God, "Please, forgive me," we let go of these age-old projections of a judging God and reconnect to a God of love and forgiveness—a true Heavenly Father. It brings about a deep feeling of relief and surrender. We feel reconnected to divine love, and we lose the sense of isolation and separation created by our own fears and judgments.

STEP 5:
Asking for Forgiveness from Oneself

Last, we ask for forgiveness from ourselves. In doing this, we resign from our 24/7 job of inner judge of our actions. We reconnect to that part of us that's always "doing our best," like a loving kid desperately trying to please his or her parents.

Yes, we make mistakes. Yes, we are imperfect when compared with our ideal of perfection. Yes, we sometimes fall short of our ideals, goals, and expectations. So what? Do we blame a toddler for not being able to walk perfectly the first time they stand up? Does it help at all to judge and criticize ourselves so harshly?

Why should we not love ourselves every step of the way as we grow and change throughout life? Do we have to wait for the end—if there is even such a thing in our endless evolution through this and perhaps other lifetimes—when we're told we'll reach perfection at last? Isn't self-love a better way to bring about progress and improvement in our lives than blame, accusation, and judgments? Why not have a good laugh at our mistakes and shortcomings for a change? Self-forgiveness comes last in the Gift of Forgiveness practice, but it is of primary importance. Like the keystone of an arch, which holds it up and strengthens it, self-forgiveness supports and strengthens the structure of our daily life. It is the keystone supporting the whole architecture of the Gift of Forgiveness.

Remember: the impact you feel from others' judgments is in direct proportion to the severity of the judgments you make about yourself. If you judge yourself a lot, the judgments of others will echo your own and have a powerful influence on you. Conversely, if you have little or no judgments towards yourself, the judgments of others will move freely through, without striking a chord in you.

Similarly, if you can't forgive yourself, you will have a hard time believing that other people, or even God, could possibly forgive you; whereas, if you forgive yourself, it will seem perfectly natural to you that others, including the Devil and God, might forgive you as well.

Your inner beliefs set the tone for others: you are the only one who can determine the positive or negative power any outside person or energy (including the divine and evil ones) holds over you. Others are only mirrors, reflecting how you love or judge yourself. If they direct an energy towards you that is not present in you, it will simply pass through you. For example, if you don't judge or hate yourself, other people's judgments and hate will not ring a bell in you. Alternatively, if you don't love and forgive yourself, you may find yourself having a hard time being receptive to the love and forgiveness you receive from other people.

So, this last step of self-forgiveness is really crucial. It comes at the end to leave us enough time to prepare ourselves slowly for the final, most important action. Usually, by the time we reach that final stage of the process, we've been so humbled by the preceding steps, we've let go of so many tensions and judgments, that this ultimate phase will be the natural consequence of the preceding ones. It is like a beautiful rose that can only come into full bloom after the stem, leaves, and bud of the flower have already grown.

STEP 6:
Expressing Gratitude

I like to start and finish each day by saying "thank you." Likewise, I like to end my practice of the Gift of Forgiveness by expressing words and thoughts of deep gratitude. In Teotihuacan, these feelings were directed toward Don Miguel, for having given me this precious gift and having made me go through the process for the first time. When I do it all by myself, I express gratitude towards life, towards God, towards the people from whom I've just asked for forgiveness, towards all the teachers from whom I've learned major lessons in my life, towards my family, my friends, and all my dear ones. Saying "thank you" opens the heart even wider; it is the simplest prayer of all. Saying "thank you" humbles us and connects us with our inner child. Find your own words of gratitude, your own reasons for saying "thank you," and let your heart sing songs of gratefulness and acknowledgment.

You may then go to sleep, if you have done this process before going to bed, or just go back to your activities, if you did it in the middle of the day. In the latter case, I would like to share with you a beautiful prayer that was given to me by Bashistya Shivananta, an inspired Indian sage. It will help you set a powerful positive intention in all of your interactions with others:

Wherever I lay my eyes,
may hope be revived and consciousness settle in.
Wherever I lay my hand,
may life generous and abundant circulate anew.
Wherever I go,
may happiness come flooding.
Wherever I am seated,
may truth show through.
Wherever I reside,
may there be Light!

CHAPTER 6

Questions
and Answers

Several questions come up regularly when I share the Gift of Forgiveness with others. I've tried to address the most common questions below, but if, after reading the following, your question has not been answered, in the spirit of this book, I beg your forgiveness!

Q: If, during this process, I ask for forgiveness from someone who has done something really wrong to me, am I not letting them get away with it?

A: The Gift of Forgiveness is intended to free you from the chains of anger, resentment, fear, or vengefulness that restrict your heart and hinder your overall capacity to love. First and foremost, it is an inner process you work with to relieve your own suffering.

The Gift of Forgiveness is designed to liberate you from the prison of your negative feelings, not from justice. If you have to take legal action against someone because of something you have suffered at their hands, you can and should do it, if you feel so inclined. But if, before taking action in the outside world, you take time to practice the

Gift of Forgiveness first, you will act from a place of inner balance and peace, not from a place of resentment, hate, or revenge. And that makes a huge difference!

No lawsuit or trial is going to bring you inner peace and contentment, even if your abuser is found guilty and you are financially compensated for their wrongdoings. The practice of the Gift of Forgiveness can be used to assist you in reaching a balanced emotional state that will allow you to recover, aside from any legal measures you consider appropriate.

The important thing here is to distinguish between *inner process* and *outer procedures.* These are two different things. Do the inner work you need to restore your balance, to heal your wounds, to be whole again. And, if needed, take the outer steps that are right.

In its highest form, love is not a feeling; it is a state of consciousness. And from that state of consciousness, you can undertake anything you feel appropriate, even if that means being very firm, uncompromising, and severe.

There is a lot of misunderstanding nowadays around the issue of "unconditional love" and the idea of "loving one's enemies." The love we are talking about here is not emotional, affective, or sentimental love. It is free of negative feelings and emotions, a mind-set (or soul-set). It allows you to see the wrongdoer as a full person, with light and darkness, without reducing that person to their worst actions, and from that consciousness to take whatever measures are appropriate to the situation. Unfortunately, examples of this kind of love are rare; hence, many people tend to adopt an attitude of love and forgiveness that is little more than outer sentimentality, a pose. This is quite different from the genuine, heartfelt kind of love and forgiveness we connect with when we practice the Gift of Forgiveness.

You can use the practice of the Gift of Forgiveness for your own well-being, without having to actively "like" all the persons from whom you ask for forgiveness. Nor do you have to give up seeking legal redress or other measures, if you deem them necessary. To illustrate this seemingly paradoxical attitude, let me share with you a joke that seems quite appropriate here:

Husband to wife: "Darling, if we didn't have our 24-room castle, our house on the West Coast, our ranch in Colorado, the two jets, the Rolls Royce, the chauffeur, the cook and maid, and our fantastic yacht on the Côte d'Azur, would you still love me?"

Wife: "Why, darling, of course I'd still love you … But I'd miss you so much!"

See? Our inner state of being doesn't have to express itself only through outer agreed and conventional behavior patterns.

Q: How many times or how often should I practice the Gift of Forgiveness?

A: Every morning and every night, for the rest of your life. No, just kidding! You don't need to follow any rules on this. Usually, though, the first few times you work with the issue of forgiveness, you may want to use it intensely and regularly during the next few days or weeks. As mentioned before, a single session will probably not be enough to deal with all the "unfinished business" you may have been carrying for a long time. Later on, you may go weeks and months without feeling the need to use it.

On the other hand, you may find that you have such a powerful experience the first time you use the Gift of Forgiveness, you don't feel the need to go back to it for a long time. Just pay attention to what happens inside you, be honest with yourself, and you will know when and how often to use it.

Q: **I neither believe in the Devil nor God. What do I make of this part of the process?**

A: It may be helpful to think of the Devil as our most negative projection and God as our most positive projection. All of us make projections, even the most "conscious" and "aware" people: the only difference here is that we are more "aware" of our projections.

In the Kabbalah, these words are written: "Before the world was created, the face wasn't looking at the face." It is a way of saying that Creation is a projection—a mirror that allows the Creator to know themself. We seem to need to project outside ourselves those things that are inside us: on other people, on Nature, on images of God, the Devil, and so on. To know and integrate these things, this projection is apparently necessary.

Even if you don't believe in the Devil or in God, you probably consider yourself to be influenced by (or even the victim of) some major outer forces, both positive and negative. We know it by many names: good or bad luck, fate, destiny, chance, hazards, "others," "Nature," "circumstances," among other things.

So, before starting the Gift of Forgiveness practice, try to identify the impersonal forces to which you give your power, the same ones you later blame when things go wrong or don't turn out the way you wanted. If you find that too complicated and difficult, when you reach that part of the process, you can simply ask for forgiveness from all impersonal outer factors, whatever they are, that you use to justify shutting yourself off and diminishing the natural flow of your love.

The idea is to reclaim responsibility for our capacity to love. When asking for forgiveness from others, from the Devil and from God, we are actually saying: "Forgive me for having blamed you for my own unconscious choice to no longer love or to love less, for having made you responsible for something that I, and only I, have power to change." We can use people, events, circumstances, Nature, abstract concepts, and beliefs to justify the fact that we've shut ourselves down.

Whatever screen we use for our projections matters little: the important thing is to reclaim these projections, to take back responsibility for our choices, and to stop blaming outside factors for things that are within our own control. If the Devil and God don't belong to the various screens you use for your own projections, it doesn't really matter. The object is to work with the impersonal factors you use habitually to feel victimized and, hence, to lessen your love.

Q: How do I know whether the people from whom I ask for forgiveness really forgive me?

A: Remember, the key to the Gift of Forgiveness is the change in state it brings about in you. Instead of placing yourself above others, so that you can judge them and grant forgiveness, you reverse the situation: you ask *them* to forgive *you*. The turnaround is what creates healing and reopens your heart.

This notion is not exclusive to Don Miguel's work. Author Byron Katie, in the powerful method of self-inquiry detailed in her book *The Work*, frequently uses such turnarounds to achieve the same ends. For instance, if someone feels negative emotions, because they think, "My dad is always judging me," Byron Katie will suggest such turnarounds as "I am always judging my dad," or "My dad is never judging me." This frees the mind from its habitual patterns of thinking, which in turns frees the heart to start loving again.

In many cases, people you judge may not even be aware that you have reason to ask for forgiveness because they may not be fully aware that you are judging, blaming, or accusing them of something. Even if they are aware of your negative feelings, given the society we live in, they may find nothing strange in such negativity and brush it off. But if you practice the Gift of Forgiveness at home and ask someone specific to forgive you, you may be surprised to find that, next time you see that person, something has changed in their attitude towards you, as a result of your own "change of heart."

So, whether the people from whom you ask forgiveness actually forgive you, the Gift of Forgiveness will work for you and may even change these people's attitude towards you.

Conclusion

I wish you much joy in working with the Gift of Forgiveness. It is a simple tool. There aren't any risks or dangers in using it, even for those of you who may be tempted to overstate its power and efficiency. You don't need special knowledge or prior experience for it to be effective. And if you devote time to this practice, I can attest to the fact that it will have an extremely positive influence on your life.

We wash our hands and take showers on a regular basis because, however careful we may be, our activities make us dirty and not always sweet-smelling. Likewise, the Gift of Forgiveness offers our heart the cleansing energy of love and forgiveness, when we have let too much emotional "dirt" accumulate around it.

May you benefit from this spiritual teaching given to me and our group by Don Miguel at Teotihuacan, and find it as useful as we do in our daily lives.

The Two Counteragreements

After reading Don Miguel's books and having the opportunity to train with him in Mexico, more than a decade ago, I have continued to use the principles laid out in *The Four Agreements*, and have written numerous articles in French about the simple yet powerful Toltec tools Don Miguel teaches. It has been a mission of mine to help promote Miguel's books in France, since most book reviewers and critics there have seemed to believe the ideas not intellectual enough to merit serious consideration.

The most difficult of the Four Agreements for me were the second and third ones: "Don't take anything personally" and "Don't make assumptions." This is probably because of their negative formulation: the use of the word "Don't." Indeed, we know today that the brain—particularly our subconscious mind—has trouble understanding negative orders or, worse, does exactly what it is being told not to do. For example: warn a young boy on his bike, "Don't go towards the hole in the road," and guess what? He'll ride straight towards that hole!

Early on in my life, I developed the habit of turning my thoughts around, of reversing my point of view. At first, I did this out of sheer curiosity; but later on, I discovered that a unique viewpoint never allows you a complete view of whatever you are considering, just as a single spotlight will always produce a shadow on the other side of any object. You need at least two spotlights to avoid shadows.

So, whenever I found myself having difficulty in using the second and third Toltec Agreements, I did what I spontaneously do all the time: I reversed them. The results were so interesting, I now refer to these as "counteragreements," and, over the years, I have developed a way of working with them that others have found helpful, too.

As a complement to the Gift of Forgiveness—and as a gift of my own to you—I am sharing below my Two Counteragreements to Don Miguel's Second and Third Toltec Agreements: "Take everything personally" and "Make lots of assumptions."

FIRST COUNTERAGREEMENT:
"Take everything personally"

When I began working with The Four Agreements, I found it difficult to follow the Second Agreement, "Don't take anything personally." Really, how do you do that? Sure, I followed Don Miguel's instructions, in which he explains that what people say about you really has nothing to do with you. But for me, there has been a hidden danger in adopting that approach, particularly if it is applied in too simplistic a manner: It can lead some people to create a sort of bubble around themselves.

Certainly, this bubble means that none of what other people do or say affects us negatively. The danger with this approach, though, is that some of us may end up out of touch with others altogether! "Not taking things personally" doesn't mean *not to take them at all*. We are not meant to make ourselves impervious to others' words nor for their actions to slide off us like water off a duck's back.

I realized that when I take something personally, it is always because others' judgments and negative comments are triggering my own judgments about myself. It's like hitting a D chord on a string guitar and causing the same chord to vibrate in other string instruments in the room; it's a type of sympathetic resonance. My reactions to what others said or did were actually showing me where I still held judgments against myself. Used appropriately, these reactions could actually assist me in identifying my inner judgments and enable me to free myself from them.

So, I decided to "Take everything personally," to deliberately let my buttons be pushed by others, to make no effort to stop myself from reacting to what others said or did. When I did this, I became acutely aware of what was triggered in me. Once I had identified a judgment against myself—the inner reason for my reaction to outer triggers—I used the Toltec tools Don Miguel describes in the *Four Agreements Companion Book*, as well as other methods I've learned over the years, to free myself of these inner judgments.

I started by identifying the origin of my self-judgment. We tend to judge ourselves in the same ways that parents, teachers, and other authority figures have judged us, when we were young. As a child, I had no choice but to accept the labels that adults stuck on me, but now, as a grown-up, I can see these judgments were biased, partial, and untrue. Others' judgments always are; no one can be 100-percent objective about us. When I realize this, I reclaim the power I gave others to judge me and no longer let anyone but myself define me.

I found that every time I was able to identify and free myself from one of these self-judgments, I simultaneously freed myself from reacting to similar judgments from others.

The counteragreement "Take everything personally" is a way to identify the ways other people mirror our negativity towards ourselves. Other people's opinions and judgments have power over us only in so much as they reflect the same attitudes in ourselves. Musically speaking, we empower others to impact us negatively by holding on to negative chords in ourselves that resonate with someone in our environment vibrating at the same frequency.

When we choose not to listen to a particular negative chord inside us, and focus instead on a more positive one, we change the way we resonate with others. Negative outer tones no longer trigger anything in us; instead, they flow through our being, without affecting us at all. We can still tune into negative vibrations and learn something from them (if only another's perspective about us), but we are no longer affected on a personal level, since we no longer have that judgment against ourselves.

There is something delightful in moving from being afraid to take things personally—and focusing on not doing so—to being open to reacting personally to what people do and say. We may even end up consciously inviting such reactions, in order to learn something about ourselves and receive clues that help us attain greater inner freedom. We might wonder: "What will I learn today from my interactions with my partner, family members, and colleagues? What kind of reactions are they going to trigger in me?" Our reactions are no longer something to fear, a sign of our "not being spiritual or evolved enough." Instead, we welcome them as symptoms of what needs healing and resolution inside us. We can have fun with this.

This approach may not be for everyone. But remember: Spiritual truths and tools are like delicious, life-giving fruits. If someone gives you a sweet, juicy peach, you're not going to frame it and hang it on your wall, nor will you put it on your private altar and burn incense sticks and pray in front of it. No. You will joyously bite into it, plant your teeth in it, savor its juice and flavor, and chew its flesh into tiny pieces that you will swallow. Then, your digestive system will sort this food out, so that you'll end up assimilating the living elements of that peach that you need (vitamins, sugar, minerals) and rejecting through your urine and feces those you don't need. The spiritual truths offered to us are meant to undergo much the same process. We must joyously taste them, extract their life-giving energies and aromas, and sort through what we are taking in, according to our own structure and needs. We then assimilate that which is useful to us and eliminate the parts that our organism, our inner being, cannot integrate.

This is what any genuine teacher or spiritual master expects from his students, apprentices, or disciples. It is also a good antidote to cult-like behavior that ends up harming both the teacher and their fanatical devotees.

SECOND COUNTERAGREEMENT:
"Make lots of assumptions"

Don Miguel's Second Agreement—"Don't make assumptions"—was even harder for me than the Third Agreement. Me, not make assumptions? You've got to be kidding! Better to ask a monkey not to pull faces. I make assumptions all the time.

Of course, there are lots of situations in which I can indeed stop making assumptions, and I have used the Third Agreement to do just that. For instance, instead of assuming what someone thinks or intends to do, I can just *ask* him/her what they truly think or are intent on doing. This can help us avoid many problems and conflicts that arise just because we assume what is going on in other people's minds and hearts, instead of just asking.

But there are also numerous situations in which we *cannot* ask the reason behind others' actions. I cannot ask all the drivers behind or in front of me why they behave on the road the way they do, for instance. I cannot ask a friend who is late, and unreachable by phone, why he is not on time. I cannot ask a political leader why he made a particular decision that impacts me in a way that I disapprove. And so on.

Naturally, when we are confronted with events in which we cannot *know* what is really happening, what are the real motivations behind what we observe, we try to *guess* and we spontaneously make assumptions about what could be the reasons and the intentions behind what we witness. However, making assumptions is not really the problem.

The problem, I came to realize, arises not in our making assumptions, plural; it arises when we make one assumption, singular, then believe that only this assumption is true. Indeed, if we are not being mindful, our first spontaneous assumption is often based on the very negative intentions we project on other people's behavior.

Instead of not making *any* assumptions—too much to ask from a mind such as mine—I resolved always to make at least two opposite assumptions in every situation, and many more if I could. For instance, a driver cuts in front of me. My first spontaneous assumption might be that he's just one more reckless driver, someone who only thinks about himself not others.

So, I immediately introduce two opposite assumptions: maybe his wife is delivering a baby on the back seat and he is rushing to the hospital; or maybe he has an asthma attack and urgently needs to get his Ventoline. You get the idea. Most importantly, by multiplying assumptions, I'm making it clear that I have no idea what really motivates his behavior. I may still find it unpleasant, of course, but I'm no longer giving in to resentment, judgments, and similar sentiments.

When we make only one assumption, our mind is projecting a negative intention behind other people's actions and, in effect, justifying the negative feeling that is triggered in us. In this way, our mind becomes the slave of our ego, and the loving overtures of our heart are drowned out by hate voices and the urge to shut down. Instead of using its full range of reflection, the mind is reduced to the status of servant to our darkest emotions. When we entertain several assumptions, the mind makes full use of its capacity to think, imagine, and reframe a situation from different angles as a means of keeping the heart open and not closed down in the face of negative reactions. In this way, our intellect can shed a great deal of light on the situation. Shining a spotlight on different areas, it prevents the heart from bogging down in cold, murky waters and coaxes it back into the warm sunshine.

As a matter of interest: some interpreters of the Bible suggest that Jesus' advice to "turn the other cheek" acknowledges an inner polarity in all of us: the intellect (thoughts, ideas) and the heart (feelings, emotions). When somebody hurts you on the left cheek—the heart—and you are overwhelmed by negative feelings, use your intellect: think, ponder, and reflect, so as to extricate yourself from the swamp of emotion. And, conversely, when you are hurt on the right cheek—the intellect—

when you are unable to think positively and your mind keeps ruminating over the same dark ideas, tune in to your heart, your feelings, and emotions: bring back warm feelings, let the flow of love water the soil of your life, which has been dessicated by mental winds.

In Greece, in ancient times, the Sophists taught their students to defend one idea, one point of view, with as convincing arguments as they could possibly find, and then, to defend the exact opposite idea or viewpoint with equal vigor. Civilized debating skills are sorely lacking in modern education. As a result, we easily become one-sided in our thinking and, held captive by our limited reactions, lose our freedom of thought in the process.

Furthermore, most, if not all, of our education system is exclusively focused on the intellect, to the detriment of the heart. We receive practically no information and no training regarding the interactions that spontaneously occur between these two aspects of ourselves. How do my feelings influence and sometimes bias my thinking? How do my thoughts trigger, justify, or counter my feelings?

In the Toltec tradition, the first mastery is the Mastery of Awareness. Indeed, if we are ever to become free, we need first to become acutely aware of what is going on within us. Learning to multiply our assumptions, as soon as anything happens that triggers an automatic negative assumption, is a simple yet powerful way to recover our intellectual and mental freedom. It allows us to be less subjugated by the negative feelings and emotions that sometimes overwhelm us.

You may find this Second Counteragreement a useful tool if you have a very powerful and quick intellect that naturally tends toward assumptions, thoughts, and reflections. The beauty of this approach is that the more you make opposite, varied, and contradictory assumptions, the less you will automatically believe any of them; you will thus deepen your capacity to give equal weight to several conflicting ideas at once. The potential payoff is enormous: the restoration of freedom of thought and, by equal measure, the freedom to choose the feelings you want to hold in your heart. Now that's true liberation.

These Two Counteragreements dovetail with hidden teachings in Don Miguel's Toltec Wisdom tradition and the traditions of a number of spiritual teachers. The opposite of a truth often holds another truth, some sages say. What's more, you don't have to choose either the original agreement or its counter form: you may pick and choose, according to your preference, using one method one day and another the next.

I have chosen not to come up with Counteragreements for the First Agreement ("Be impeccable with your word") or the Fourth Agreement ("Always do your best"). I didn't feel it was necessary, as I enjoy practicing these Agreements just the way they are. Impeccability of speech—however difficult it may be to practice at times—is part of many spiritual teachings and is something I have long tried to put into practice. A superb example of the power of impeccability of speech, to my mind, is Maître Philippe de Lyon, one of the 20th century's greatest healers. Sometimes called the "unknown master," Maître de Lyon always asked for the same "payment" from the people he cured: "Don't speak ill of others for [depending on the patient] … a day … a week … a month … or longer." That says a lot about the power of this First Agreement, I believe.

Likewise, I use the Fourth Agreement just as it is. I remember Marshall Rosenberg, founder of Nonviolent Communication (NVC), making an interesting turnaround of a famous

English proverb that goes, "If something is worth doing, it's worth doing well." Marshall liked to say, "Anything worth doing at all is worth doing badly." His meaning? That if something is really worth doing, then it's worth trying to do it no matter what, even if you don't do it well.

To sum up: Turnarounds and reversals can sometimes open interesting doors for us—when we feel stuck; when a particular tool, idea, or solution doesn't seem to work; and when something we hold true results in very negative thoughts and feelings.

In Chinese Taoism, the circular, black-and-white, yin-yang symbol reminds us that, in Nature, harmony comes from the interplay of different energies of equal merit. Tigers and elephants, for instance, have their own power at the top of the food chain, but so, too, do viruses and microbes at the bottom of the chain, which although infinitely smaller, nevertheless can weaken or kill creatures many times larger than themselves. Power is always evenly distributed between opposite polarities.

Therefore, when we feel powerless, it may be that it is time for us to try the opposite solution to the one we've been using so far. Life keeps inviting us not to limit ourselves, to explore farther, to keep moving on and progressing. This progression is endless, so that as soon as we start believing that "we're there," that we've reached our destination, a new road is already opening up in front of us. Isn't that wonderful?

I wish you the best on your own path!

Acknowledgments

A big, warm thank you to Don Miguel Ruiz: I appreciate not only the precious Gift of Forgiveness you gave me but also the memorable days we spent in Mexico and the heart wisdom you so generously share in your books. More than words alone, your simple manner and way of life have been an example to me. You "walk your talk."

A big thank you to Maud Séjournant: for introducing Don Miguel's books to me; for giving me the opportunity to translate and publish them in French; for arranging for me to to meet Don Miguel in Mexico and, later, Brandt Morgan in New Mexico; and, last but not least, for all the other books and projects we've collaborated on over the years.

Thank you, Brandt Morgan: for being such a fine Toltec mentor and a true spiritual brother: I learned a lot about Toltec wisdom from you in New Mexico, the week that followed our encounter with Don Miguel, and I am deeply thankful for this. Like the rest of our 1999 group, I was lucky to be there, in Santa Fe, when you suddenly found the inspiration to create the "Walk of Vision" and to be the first to experience it on the grounds of the ranch where we were staying. (I still remember the answer I got to the first question I asked.) I am glad that, through your lovely book, this powerful tool is now available to French- and English-speaking readers.

Thank you to all the participants of the 1999 Teotihuacan group, particularly Gérard, Maria-Elena, Virginie, Anne, Jacqueline, and Alexandrine: This experience would not have been the same without your presence, your qualities, your humor, and your love.

"Last, but no least", as they say, a warm "Merci !" to Thierry Bogliolo, my publisher at Findhorn Press, for having so promptly accepted this book of mine, and to Nicky Leach, my editor, for having done such a great job at improving my English and rephrasing sentences: more than that, I was lucky to benefit from her years of writing experience and expertise which, as a frequent editor myself for French authors, I appreciate for their genuine value.

About the Author

Born and raised in Geneva, Switzerland, Olivier Clerc presently lives in southern Burgundy, France, with his beloved partner and three sons. He works as a writer, translator, and editorial consultant, specializing in spirituality, shamanism, personal development, transpersonal psychology and human relationships.

Olivier has crossed paths with many famous authors and teachers, whose books he has translated into French, and with whom he has often trained. Among them are Marshall Rosenberg, founder of Nonviolent Communication; Toltec master and author Don Miguel Ruiz; Dr. Stanislav Grof, a psychiatrist with more than forty years' experience of research into non-ordinary states of consciousness and one of the founders and chief theoreticians of transpersonal psychology; Robert Monroe, researcher into altered consciousness and founder of The Monroe Institute; and many others.

He began his writing career at the age of 20, when his first book, on lucid dreaming, found an enthusiastic audience. He is the author of eight books, including two other titles published in the United States: *Modern Medicine: The New World Religion*: *How Beliefs Secretly Influence Medical Dogmas and Practices* (Personhood Press, 2004) and *Invaluable Lessons from a Frog: Seven Life-Enhancing Metaphors* (Dreamriver Press, 2009).

For more information please visit Olivier's Web site *www. olivierclerc.com*—you will find a short descriptive section in English there.

Recommended Reading

CLERC, OLIVIER. *Modern Medicine: The New World Religion*: *How Beliefs Secretly Influence Medical Dogmas and Practices*. Translation by Rachel Stern. Fawnskin, CA: Personhood Press. 2004.

CLERC, OLIVIER. *Invaluable Lessons from a Frog: Seven Life-Enhancing Metaphors*. Flourtown, PA: Dreamriver Press. 2009.

KATIE, BYRON AND STEPHEN MITCHELL. *Loving What Is: Four Questions That Can Change Your Life*. New York, NY: Three Rivers Press. 2003.

MORGAN, BRANDT. *Vision Walk: Asking Questions, Getting Answers, Shifting Consciousness*. Pittsburgh, PA: St. Lynn's Press. 2006.

NELSON, MARY CARROLL AND DON MIGUEL RUIZ. *Beyond Fear: A Toltec Guide to Freedom and Joy: The Teachings of Don Miguel Ruiz*. Tulsa, OK: Council Oak Books. 1997.

ROSENBERG, MARSHALL. *Nonviolent Communication*: *A Language of Life*. Encinitas, CA: PuddleDancer Press. 2003.

RUIZ, DON MIGUEL. *The Four Agreements: A Practical Guide to Personal Freedom*. A Toltec Wisdom Book. San Rafael, CA: Amber-Allen Publishing. 1997.

RUIZ, DON MIGUEL. *Mastery of Love: A Practical Guide to the Art of Relationship*. A Toltec Wisdom Book. San Rafael, CA: Amber-Allen Publishing. 1999.

RUIZ, DON MIGUEL AND JANET MILLS. *The Voice of Knowledge: A Practical Guide to Inner Peace*. A Toltec Wisdom Book. San Rafael, CA: Amber-Allen Publishing. 2004.

RUIZ, DON MIGUEL AND JANET MILLS. *The Four Agreements Companion Book: Using the Four Agreements to Master the Dream of Your Life*. A Toltec Wisdom Book. San Rafael, CA: Amber-Allen Publishing. 2000.

SÉJOURNANT, MAUD. *Le Cercle de Vie: Initiation Chamanique d'Une Psychothérapeute*. Paris: Albin Michel. 1997.

F I N D H O R N   P R E S S

Life-Changing Books

Consult our catalogue online
(with secure order facility) on
www.findhornpress.com

For information on the Findhorn Foundation:
www.findhorn.org

The Five Agreements Game

by Olivier Clerc,

Marc Kucharz & Brandt Morgan

A CHIVALRY OF RELATIONSHIPS

Use the power of the Five Agreements to transform your life - to become completely happy and free.

The Five Agreements can transform your life by replacing the thousands of self-limiting beliefs that ruin your relationships with yourself, others and life itself. In the book that comes with this game, Olivier Clerc introduces the Toltec way as an authentic "chivalry" of relationships, allowing us to establish impeccable relationships with both others and ourselves. Simply playing this game will lead you to use the five simple yet efficient agreements to fully accept yourself and others. Thus you will acquire self-mastery in three major steps.

Boxed game · ISBN 978-1-84409-617-6

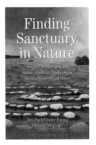

Finding Sanctuary in Nature

by Jim PathFinder Ewing

SIMPLE CEREMONIES IN THE NATIVE AMERICAN
TRADITION FOR HEALING YOURSELF AND OTHERS

Finding Sanctuary in Nature takes the reader through a series of
teachings designed to awaken an appreciation of the spiritual forces
at large in the world using shamanic techniques found in Native
American spirituality. Included are hands-on exercises, step-by-step
instructions for ceremonies, and notebook items from the author's
own life. *Finding Sanctuary in Nature* takes *Clearing*, the author's
first book, to the next level—from clearing spaces of unwanted
energies to creating sacred spaces within which to perform simple
ceremonies for healing oneself and others. All the tools one needs
to start performing ceremonies are provided in this book, from the
"whys" and "hows" to the basic teachings, with dozens of ceremonies explained. Learn how to:

- Connect with spirit guides and angels • Interpret symbols
- Make a medicine wheel and use it as an engine for distance healing
Create ceremonies for daily living • Return an individual's lost soul
pieces (soul retrieval) • Heal the Earth and much more

192 pages paperback, 9 line drawings · ISBN 978-1-84409-095-2

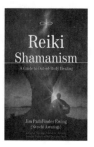

Reiki Shamanism

by Jim PathFinder Ewing

A GUIDE TO OUT-OF-BODY HEALING

Learn how to heal people, places, and things, whether at hand or from a distance. Presented by an expert in both traditions, the techniques of Reiki and the principles of shamanism are explained in simple, concise terms, then brought together using real-life examples to show how Reiki can be practiced within the shamanic journey.

Supported by mastery exercises, references to other books, and internet resources, both novices and experienced practitioners will expand their knowledge and ability to help subjects clear old energies and accelerate their "soul purpose."

"Weaving the energy medicine of Reiki with the ancient healing power of shamanic journeying, *Reiki Shamanism* illuminates the pathway to a completely new level of spiritual insight and healing ability. Recommended to anyone seeking to develop their inner abilities of healing and understanding."
—**MICHAEL DRAKE, author of** *The Shamanic Drum*

192 page paperback, line drawings · ISBN 978-1-84409-133-1

Clearing

by Jim PathFinder Ewing

A GUIDE TO LIBERATING ENERGIES
TRAPPED IN BUILDINGS AND LANDS

Working from the premise that every natural and human-made space has an energy of its own that can physically and emotionally affect anyone in that space, this introduction to ancient practices of environmental shamanism—or transformation of the energy of spaces—explains in practical terms how to liberate old, unproductive energy that may be stored in any space, making room for new vibrations to circulate and increase inhabitants well-being. Real-life examples, guided exercises, annotated endnotes, and an extensive glossary to supplement case studies are also included.

"*Clearing* is an excellent primer for the compassionate clearing of dead energy. Filled with explanations and examples to help in the process, this pocket companion is a must read for anyone interested in helping to heal the earth."
—**KATHLEEN JACOBY**, author of *Vision of the Grail*

128 pages paperback · ISBN 978-1-84409-082-2